EXTINCTION

(On the Edge)

A One Act Play

Lynn C Campbell

Dedicated to Don & Alex

Note from the Playwright

First written and performed more than twenty years ago, this play, 'Extinction' consumed me - it's ideas and truths still captivate me, and remain strikingly relevant today.

Performed in 1993 with the Mount Gambier Theatre Group, my vision reached the stage. Heartfelt thanks to Wendy Bonny for her inspiration and for composing most of the music, with two pieces by Rob Barton; the music was/is amazing. My gratitude also to the performers who brought my surreal vision to life and to Jean Cameron for believing in me.

In the script, the court session is adjourned for 20 years. That time has passed. It is now time to reopen the case. I therefore challenge you to provide new evidence to support the upcoming trial.

Lynn C Campbell

Writer, Director, Publisher

Music/Sound

On the Edge - Instrumental	- Rob Barton
Johann Strauss II	- Excerpt
On the Ice Shelf	- Wendy Bonny - Ragtime / Polka
Imminent Extinction	- Wendy Bonny - Reggae/Gospel
Mad Man Yorick	- Popular tune (Do wah diddy)
Science Rap	- Wendy Bonny
Times Past	- Wendy Bonny
Harmony	- Wendy Bonny
Ecological Crawl	- Rob Barton, Wendy Bonny
Harmony/Music/Lyrics	

Note: LX, FX and SFX - most have been left up to the Director's creative vision. In some instances, directions have been left in for clarification.

This book is copyright, apart from any fair dealing for the purpose of private study, research, or review, as permitted under the Copyright Act, no part may be reproduced by any process without written permission. Inquiries concerning publication translation or recording rights should be addressed to the publisher.

Any performance or public reading of Extinction is forbidden unless a license has been received from the author or the author's agent. The purchase of this book in no way gives the purchaser the right to perform the play in public, whether by means of a stage production or a reading.

All applications for public performance should be addressed to:

carolecampbell390@gmail.com

Synopsis

The quest for power, money and self-survival are presented to a judge and jury for trial. Extinction is discussed and the opinions of how some people have a disregard for vegetation and wildlife. It is the year 1991, set in a World Courtroom with the Government of the day in power. All comments made by the Pope and Newsreader is recorded fact.

The genre is epic theatre, demonstrating didacticism. Alienation techniques in the form of popular music, lyrics and slides provide evidence when the world is put on trial. Although the play has a strong moral message on the environment, over-the-top humour is the element used to entertain the audience. It has a large cast with many opportunities for actors to double up. It is also suitable for educational purposes.

Choreographed penguins in a song and dance routine swim to shore to the music from a section of Johann Strauss II Emperor Waltz; other music is ragtime, reggae, gospel and heavy metal. Also, there is a science rap, 50's Rock meltdown. Props required for the performance are minimal. All lyrics were written by Lynn Campbell with the exception of Harmony by Wendy Bonny.

News Panel

The news panel provides factual information, juxtaposed with slides as a presentation onto the cyclorama. However, a newsreader may serve the same purpose by providing further information, announcing the events taking place.

Costumes

For the initial production the penguins were stylised wearing black tails, white shirts and tights and yellow bow ties. The gorillas were dressed in dungarees, striped shirts and beanies. Seagulls wore white 'T' shirts, shorts and red socks. The bugs wore black tops and bottoms in various styles, tinsel wigs and sunglasses. Futuristic people were dressed in white long 'T' shirts and white tights with bright coloured sashes around the waist. Note: Theocratic Counsel is an angel representing theocracy and was made to look like a Christmas tree decoration.

Props

The world panel or members of the jury use basic props to represent nations, peoples and birds; for example, cardboard seagulls, hats, coats, bandanas etc. Dr Sciencestein carries various items such as, a globe, blackboard and chalk, magnifying glass and pointer, insecticide spray gun and cardboard plane.

Lighting & Special Effects

The aim is to create a surrealistic world; hot and cold environments. The use of the cyclorama and other tech' equipment such as ultra violet light, along with strobe helps create a slow-motion panic effect during 'Melt Down' and also during the final slide of Chernobyl, to create a strong alienation effect when the futuristic people die. A mirror ball may also be used to create stars. For the first performance, all materials used were recycled, with a grand total cost of $12 for production.

Set Requirements

Three seats, rostrum and lectern for the Judiciary. Two bench seats for world participants. Slide projector and stand or overhead projector. Chair and microphone for the newsreader if used instead of a News Panel; Slides/PowerPoint.

Suggested Slides

1. The Ross Ice Shelf
2. Rusted Junk In Antarctica
3. Expeditionists in Antarctica, relaxing
4. Penguins in Antarctica
5. Rain Forest
6. Wood Chipper
7. Zaire Forest
8. Bohemian Rain Forest (out of existence)
9. Endangered Species
    Slides 9 - 19 various endangered species/Water Cycle Diagram
20. Deforestation in China
21. Disposable Chopsticks
22. Soldier on burning Kuwait beach
23. Boy in Cuba Tao – Valley of Death
24. Deforestation
25. Forest Destruction
26. Soil Erosion
27. Soil Salinity
28. Death of a River
29. Ramshackle
30. A solitary tree on barren land
31. Damage caused by soil erosion
32. More salinity
33. Mother and child; third world poverty
34. Burnt Sand in Kuwait
35. Chernobyl Disaster

Theocracy v's Democracy

The Court is Inquisitional. A Judge wears a wig and a scarlet-coloured robe; he is quite mad. High Counsel is also wigged and gowned. Theocratic Counsel is dressed like an Angel off a Christmas tree. Dr Sciencestein wears a white lab' coat and has electrifying hair; he speaks with a German accent and is comically crazy. The Prosecution comprises of Judge, High Counsel and Theocratic Counsel. A large projector or PowerPoint provides evidence. Opposite is the World Panel or Defense which consists of three members to represent different world participants and perspectives. Democratic Counsel is part of this contingent and Dr Sciencestein also joins the world panel at times.

The Judge attempts to view the facts as presented without prejudice to either claim. Theocratic Counsel acts on behalf of the Almighty Presence for world prosecution and supremacy. High Counsel acts as mediator between the events presented between Theocratic and Democratic Counsel. Dr Sciencestein represents both science and sovereignty, however he is neither for theocracy or democracy but seen as a world renown leader in the field of science and technology; he also acts on behalf of all scientific bodies throughout the world.

Extinction

Scene - Courtroom - *A rostrum for the Judge and two seats positioned stage left. Two bench seats stage right for the jury or World Panel. To the far right, in front of the House Curtain is the Newsreader who remains there for the whole performance. The Cyclorama – to depict mood, temperature or place for various events. Dr Sciencestein enters erratically when required from various entrances.*

Enter P: **World Panel.**

Enter OP: **High Counsel and Judge**

Enter OP: **Theocratic Counsel.**

HIGH COUNSEL: [*To World Panel.*] All rise. Be seated.

Noisy discussion between World Panel.

HIGH COUNSEL: Order! Order! [*Bangs gavel.*]

JUDGE: This court of conjecture is now in session. World Members charged please stand. Higher Powers vs World at Large. The World is hereby charged with the following offences: rape, pillaging, looking out for self and financial gain, forest destruction, death to beasts of the fields. The consequences of these actions predict extinction. How do you plead?

WORLD PANEL: Not guilty Your Honour!

JUDGE: Due to the seriousness of these allegations, I have insisted evidence be presented in detail from world members.

HIGH COUNSEL: Be seated. I now call upon Exhibit A.

Slide 1: The Ross Ice Shelf

DEMOCRATIC COUNSEL: Your Honour! We are fully aware that Antarctica is now under threat. The main international instrument for the management of the continent is the Antarctic Treaty of 1959 which provides for such matters of the use of the region exclusively for peaceful purposes. We have since introduced a proposal . . .

Enter **Dr Sciencestein**

DR SCIENCESTEIN: Ah yes. CRAMRA. The proposal for a Convention on the 'Regulation of Antarctic Mineral Resource Activities'.

JUDGE: What? What? What?

HIGH COUNSEL: This proposal was tabled in Parliament, November 1988, Your Honour.

DR. SCIENCESTEIN: Australia lays claim to 42% of the Antarctic Continent.

'The Emperor Waltz'. [Johann Strauss II – *Choreographed swim to shore.*]

Enter **Penguin 1, Penguin 2, Penguin 3, Baby Penguin,** [*Swim to shore.*]

Slide 2: Rusted Junk in Antarctica *Penguin dialogue - inflated English voice.*

PENGUIN 1: What is that?

PENGUIN 2: It's a piece of rusted junk.

PENGUIN 3: Didn't you see the miners digging today?

PENGUIN 1: There are easier ways to catch fish.

PENGUIN 2: No silly. They're looking for minerals. [*Jokes.*] As usual, America wants to be in the Guinness book of records as the world's first.

PENGUIN 1: [*Sighs.*] It's much more peaceful and not so hostile at the Amery Ice Shelf.

PENGUIN 2: Isn't that where the Aussie Science laboratories are?

PENGUIN 3: They lay claim to almost half of our home and have warned miners to stay away.

ALL: Jolly good. Jolly good.

PENGUIN 1: Sounds strange to me.

Enter **Bruce** [*Waddling to the group.*]

PENGUIN 3: Speak of the devil. Here comes Bruce.

BRUCE: G'day

PENGUIN 1: Is it? There are all sorts of strange goings on here, I can tell you.

BRUCE: Come over to the Ice Palace with me and Sheila. She'll be right mate; they won't bother you there.
PENGUIN 3: Think you're pretty cool don't you? Anyway, what's so scary about the Amery Ice Shelf?

BRUCE: Nothing really, only some guy called 'Bill' banned exploration and mining.

Assembling on the Ice Shelf - *Reggae/Polka Penguins*

> We can endure an arctic winter
> Breed in hostile conditions
> Assembling on the ice shelf
> Keeping warm, keeping warm.
>
> It's icy cold and it's freezing
> Where we do all our breeding,
> We can't do any nesting
> Feet are warm, feet are warm.
>
> In our natural deep freeze,
> Our chick is incubating
> Bellies huddled over
> Toasty warm, toasty warm

And when our little chicken hatches
We both feed and rear it
Assembling on the Ice Shelf
Keeping warm, keeping warm

Enter **Australia - Greenies** [*Carrying placards and shouting opinions.*]

NEWS PANEL: 60 MILLION DOLLARS IS SPENT EACH YEAR FROM TAXPAYER'S MONEY IN THE NAME OF SCIENCE AND SOVEREIGNTY.

AUSTRALIA **GREENIES:** [*Shouting at adjudicators, world panel and audience.*] Quite Franklin! You! Don't give a dam!

G1: A signatory conserving flora and fauna in Antarctica!

G2: Australia claim 42% of ice water!

G3: No formal prohibition on our mining activity!

G4: A moratorium remains in place!

Enter **Dr Sciencestein**

WORLD PANEL/DR SCIENCESTEIN: Get them out of here.

General noise and disorder as **protesters** *are shoved out by the* **world panel**. *and Dr Sciencestein.*

JUDGE/HIGH COUNSEL: Order! Order!

NEWS PANEL: IN MAY '89 THE COALITION ANNOUNCED ITS OPPOSITION TO AUSTRALIA SIGNING CRAMRA. IN THE ABSENCE OF THE CONVENTION THERE IS NO FORMAL PROHIBITION ON MINING ACTIVITY BUT A MORATORIUM REMAINS IN PLACE.

PENGUIN 1: [*To Bruce.*] Give yourself a pat on the back.

PENGUIN 2: Here – if you're so smart, tell me why Australians have the worst extinction record in the world?

PENGUIN 1: Something to do with charisma? Eh!

PENGUIN 3: There's not much action and there's plenty of talking.

PENGUIN 1: It's people you know – voting in governments to make major decisions.

PENGUIN 2: Trouble is, you never know when to believe a politician. When it comes to environmental issues it sounds like they're doing their usual hot air routine and people simply shrug it off.

PENGUINS 1/2/3: Yes. Yes. Yes. Of course!

BRUCE: It's getting mighty warm here. They really are trying to get through to the Australian public.

PENGUIN 3: If they can't keep their own home in order, how can we believe they'll protect ours? Ha!

PENGUIN 2: If they upset the balance there's no way of knowing what might happen?

PENGUIN 1: Tell you what . . . if we survive this winter, we'll think about immigrating to Amery.

PENGUIN 3: It's getting quite chilly. Let's huddle.

Exit penguins.

JUDGE: What about the other countries?

DEMOCRATIC COUNSEL: Your Honour, the treaty is constantly under review.

JUDGE: It appears this situation is tenuous.

Enter **Girl**.

GIRL: Our world is bright and beautiful
    A paradise on planet earth
    Rich soil, glazed emerald carpets
    Crowned Kings, dwellers on earth
    Adorned with exotic perfumed flowers
    Soaking life's water
    Bearing abundant luxuriant fruits
    Nectar of the Gods

Exit

DEMOCRATIC COUNSEL: Tropical forests produce the finest hardwood timber. Sometimes only one type of tree is required but whole areas are clear felled to get it. The majority of men are not interested in forest management.

HIGH COUNSEL: Trees are one of the most fundamental resources of the planet. I now present Exhibit B.

Slide 5: Rain Forest

JUDGE: Dr Sciencestein, what is your scientific viewpoint on this issues?

Enter **Sciencestein**

DR SCIENCESTEIN: We are not very optimistic. [*Exit*.]

JUDGE: Hmm. Thank you Sciencestein.. High Counsel please continue.

HIGH COUNSEL: I would now like to present to your Honour, Exhibit C: The Dark Continent where wild animals exist in their natural habitat.

Scene Amazon Forest

Butterfly Puppetry.

Enter **Gorilla 1, Gorilla 2, Gorilla 3**

GORILLA 1: This is the life. Umm! This tastes good.

GORILLA 2: Let's play leapfrog!

Gorillas *have fun playing leapfrog.*

GORILLA 3: Isn't it peaceful?

Slide 6: Wood Chipper

GORILLA 2: Look over there, it's a Morebark Chipper. They've left the keys in. Anyone for a spin?

Gorillas *crank imaginary engine.*

FX *Engine running.*

Gorillas *go crazy.*

Slide 7: Zaire Forest

NEWS PANEL: THE AMAZON RAIN FOREST IS MADE UP OF SIX LAYERS WITH CHARACTERISTICS OF FLORA, FAUNA AND MICROCLIMATE.

GORILLA 1: It's nice and cool on top of these rotten leaves. Smells good too.

GORILLA 2: I like to feel the soft-stemmed herbs and seedlings.

GORILLA 3: Hey! Let's play eye-spy.

GORILLA 1: Okay! Me first! Let me see . . . something beginning with C . . .

GORILLA 2: Celery.

GORILLA 1: No.

GORILLA 3: Upper or lower parts?

GORILLA 1: Upper.

GORILLA 2: Oh, that's easy, the canopy

GORILLA 1: Nope.

GORILLA 3: I've got it! I've got it Crowns . . .

GORILLA 1: Yep! You got it. Your turn.

Gorilla 3 *goes Ape.*

GORILLA 3: [*Spying.*] Something beginning with S.

GORILLA 1: That's easy - sky.

GORILLA 3: Yes, we're seeing more and more of it every day.

GORILLA 1: I wish they'd stop harvesting.

GORILLA 2: What if these men cut down all of our trees?
    The sky hasn't got any buds or berries·

GORILLA 3: We'll all die.

GORILLA 2: They don't understand us and even if they did, they wouldn't l listen.

Slide 8: Bohemian Rain Forest

NEWS PANEL: NO ONE HAS MADE AN INVENTORY OR KNOWS HOW MANY SPECIES OR LIVING ORGANISMS LIVE IN THE TROPICS.

Slides 9 - 19 Endangered Species

Imminent Extinction - *Gorillas [Emphasis on 'who.'*

    Is there anyone out there who cares?
    Is there anyone who will - listen?
    Hear our cries and save our souls
    From - imminent extinction

    Is there anyone out there please here us?

> Is there anyone out there, at all?
> We need your help please guide our path
> From - imminent extinction
>
> The forest is our home
> A place where we can live
> We - can - live - in
> Evolved or created by a God - up - above
> God - up - above
>
> We want to live. We - want - to - live
> We want to give We - want - to - give
> Please save our souls
> From - imminent - extinction.

Slide 20: The Water Cycle Diagram

NEWS PANEL: THE DIVERSITY OF PLANT SPECIES IS REFLECTED IN THE DIVERSITY OF ANIMAL SPECIES. SOME ANIMALS NOW EXTINCT.

> Is there anyone out there?
> Please help us
> Once extinct we are gone for - ever
> You can help, please guide our souls
> From - imminent extinction

NEWS PANEL: FOR EVERY TONNE OF TIMBER IN TREES, ONE TONNE OF CARBON DIOXIDE IS ABSORBED AND ONE TONNE OF OXYGEN RELEASED. ESSENTIAL FOR RESPIRATION.

FX Distant tree felling.

GORILLA 2: Time to make scarce. They're at it again.

GORILLA 3: They might like some celery stalks. There's plenty here.

GORILLA 1: Share with humans - not a chance.

GORILLA 2: I wish they'd leave us alone.

GORILLA 1: They need the Kings to make houses to live in and to make furniture.

GORILLA 3: It sounds like an awful lot of work. Do all humans live in tree houses?

GORILLA 1: No not all. Japanese humans do.

GORILLA 2: How do you know that? You haven't been to Japan.

GORILLA 1: The yellow casqued horn-bill told me.

GORILLA 3: Don't they have a forest of their own?

GORILLA 2: Don't think so, otherwise why would they want our trees?

Enter **Japan** *from World Panel*

Slide 22 Disposable Chopsticks

JAPAN: Two thirds of Japan is covered by trees; revered by all. Trees from the Amazon are used to build Japanese houses, furniture and wooden baths as well as other items. It is the people of the Amazon that choose to strip their land not Japanese people. We are fully aware that poor countries export wood for income. However, they want the sale and we choose to buy. [*Exit to World Panel.*]

NEWS PANEL: 45 MILLION DISPOSABLE CHOPSTICKS PER MONTH SENT TO JAPAN FROM PAPUA NEW GUINEA.

Slide 23: Deforestation in China

Psychedelic Sunset - *Gorillas*

> Psychedelic sunset, circling the evening
> Stroking mountain paths and streams
> Melting in the twilight
> Darkness covered forests
> Dewy petaled flowers
> Water falling all around
> Shimmers in the breeze
>
> **NEWS PANEL** THE HIGHEST RATE OF TROPICAL DEFORESTATION IS BY BRAZIL, COLUMBIA AND ECUADOR. DEFORESTATION IS A GLOBAL ISSUE.

FX *Distant tree felling.*

Gorillas *remain lying down.*

> It's our world, blue and green
> Flowers fragrance breathing
> Feathered trees, in the breeze
> Peacefully soothing
>
> And I love life as much as I love you
> In this world of so much confusion
> Yet, how can I feel a love so real
> In a world of disillusion
>
> But I know, yes I know
> The pain and hurt that you show
> Makes me want to keep on believing
> That one special day, in our own special way
> We'll live in harmony

>   Psychedelic sunset, circling the evening
>   Stroking mountain paths and streams
>   Melting in the twilight
>   Dewy petaled flowrs
>   Water falling all around
>   Shimmers in the breeze

NEWS PANEL: SINCE 1950 THE WORLD HAS LOST OVER HALF OF ITS TREES WHICH IS MORE THAN IN THE REST OF MAN'S HISTORY.

FX Loud tree crashing

Exit **gorillas** *running.*

Enter **Dr Sciencestein**.

DR SCIENCESTEIN: An area containing half of all the growing timber in the world must represent a large proportion of the world's total pool of genetic information.

JUDGE: Hmm. Yes quite. Theocratic Counsel, what is your view?

THEOCRATIC COUNSEL: God said to all men: "Here I have given to you all vegetation bearing seed which is on the surface of the whole earth and every tree on which there is the fruit of a tree bearing seed, to you let it serve as food. And to everything moving upon the earth in which there is life as soul, I have given all green vegetation for food. *(Genesis 1:29)*

France *Steps forward from the World Panel*

FRANCE: Les forets occupant une quart de territoire nationale, qui fait de la France le plus boise d'Europ occidental.

THEOCRATIC COUNSEL: "The wise are the ones that treasure up knowledge, but the mouths of the foolish ones is near to ruin itself." *(Proverbs 10:14)*

JUDGE: Dr Sciencestein, what are your comments?

DR SCIENCESTEIN: Hmm. I wonder what Darwin would say about this? We are trying desperately to find a solution – advising populations - reuse - recycle. But, that's not the major problem. It's major industries trying to make quick bucks.

JUDGE: Quick bucks!

DR SCIENCESTEIN: Yes, your Honour. People are not prepared to give up their livelihood no matter what the cost. [*Aside.*] Of course, we do make mistakes and greed for money continues to be a major problem. We enjoy our research.

NEWS PANEL: AT THE CURRENT RATE OF DEFORESTATION, IT WILL TAKE 100 YEARS FOR THE PLANET TO BE CLEARED.

Slide 24 – 26: Boy - Cuba; Valley of Death; Deforestation; Forest Destruction

JUDGE: What do you say to that Sciencestein?

Enter **Dr Sciencestein**

Science Rap *Dr Sciencestein*

> We have a great big planet
> A giant science lab easy for the taking
> Experimenting with our CFC's
> We got to cocktail making
> Who cares? Not I.
> I'm not in that department
> When the sun goes up and the sun goes down,
> We work on new creations
>
> We have a great big planet
> A giant science lab, easy for the taking
> Mistakes are made, but what the heck
> I get my eggs and bacon
> Who cares? Not I.
> There's a profit in the making

World Panel *raise a ruckus.* HIGH COUNSEL: Order! Order!

JUDGE: Really Sciencestein!

Exit Sciencestein.

Slide – Rain Forest

Enter **All gorillas.**

FX Gun shot.

Gorilla 1 *Hit by the bullet and dies.*

Baby gorilla *Huddles close to its mother.*

Enter grotesque **Black Traders.**

1st TRADER: Got the old bag. Quick before they regroup.

2nd TRADER: Get as many as you can.

1st TRADER: Not the old ones – only the young ones.

2nd TRADER: We'll get a packet for this lot.

1st TRADER: Yeah. If they all survive.

2nd TRADER: If one survives, we're laughing. [*Grabs baby gorilla.*]

1st TRADER: Let's get out of here, the loggers are coming.

VOICE OVER: Over there. Black traders. Watch out for gunfire.

Gorillas *mournfully drag off family member.*

NEWS PANEL: MOTHERS OF ORANGUTANGS ARE KILLED IN THE INDONESIAN RAIN FORESTS. BABIES ARE SOLD ON THE BLACK MARKET FOR A MINIMUM PRICE OF $20,000 AMERICAN DOLLARS.

JUDGE: High Counsel, please continue.

HIGH COUNSEL: Your Honour, from the evidence brought before you, it is clear that men are not concerned about their own future generations.

JUDGE: Hmm! Damages you say? What do you say High Counsel?

HIGH COUNSEL: Here and now is of import and of course money. Most men display misplaced sincerity towards animal life. It is fine to destroy their habitat but it is criminal to trade them on the black market.

THEOCRATIC COUNSEL: Hypocrisy is the name of the game.

HIGH COUNSEL: [*Overly excited.*] Hear! Hear.!

WORLD MEMBERS: Objection your Honour! She/he can't say that.

HIGH COUNSEL/JUDGE: Order! Order!

JUDGE: Hypocrisy is hereby stricken from the record. Continue High Counsel

HIGH COUNSEL: On the island of Nauru, every man woman and child earn approximately thirty thousand dollars per year making super phosphate garden fertiliser from bird droppings, which have accumulated over thousands of years.

Enter **Boy** flying paper plane. He stops and looks up.

BOY: It's a plane. It's a bird. [Wipes face.] Yuk! It's super phosphate.

Enter **Seagulls**

1st SEAGULL: We've bequeathed them super phosphate and what thanks do we get?

2nd SEAGULL: As long as we can sit here, they'll leave us alone, so stop your complaining.

1st SEAGULL: Do you realise we've been hanging around here for thousands of years, long before they were here?

2nd SEAGULL: I wonder what they'll do when there's none left? Probably leave, I suppose.

1st SEAGULL: Mm.... I wonder? The fish are jumping. Care for a bite?

2nd SEAGULL: Race you back.

JUDGE: Any comments Democratic Counsel?

Democratic Counsel *steps forward from the Prosecution.*

DEMOCRATIC COUNSEL: Your Honour. Third world countries need to be made aware of the consequences of profiteering from earth's resources and be provided with appropriate management measures to protect their livelihood. It is the Western world's responsibility to pass on any information learned as it comes to hand as they are also, indubitably at risk.

Enter **Pope** *driving Pope Mobile.*

POPE: The ecological crisis is a moral issue. [*Exit.*]

DEMOCRATIC COUNSEL: Your Honour – I believe management and leadership is the key word here. I therefore call Australia to take the floor to provide evidence.

Australia *steps forward from World Panel.*

AUSTRALIA: The Hawke government identified four goals, Your Honour!

The following slides are shown throughout the jargon.

Slides 27 – 33: Soil erosion; Soil Salinity; Death of a River Ramshackle; Salinity; A solitary tree on barren land; Damage caused by soil erosion.; Australian Salinisation

90's Poly Jargon Politicians -

The rhythm of the dialogue is loosely based on 'Model Major General'. (Gilbert & Sullivan)

Enter **Pol 1** *and* **Pol 2** *P & OP, meet centre then separate right and left.*

Pol 1: Sustainable development requires specific strategy
        It must not jeopardise our health or any productivity.

Pol 2: Biological constraints maintain respectability
        For maintenance of life on planet earth

Enter **Pol 3, Pol 4**

Pol 3: Ecological sustainable development
        Conservation and enhancement issues at the present

Pol 4: In need of reclamation due to land degradation
        The pressure of life's courses depleting earth's resources

Pol 3: Now and in the future will augment

Enter **Pol 5, Pol 6**

Pol 5: South Australian politicians play at table strategy
        Creating policies, preventing soil salinity

Pol 6: Soil acidification in our crop pasture systems
        Salinisation is a problem, which will increase

Enter **Pol 7, Pol 8**

Pol 7: Industrial poisoning, pollutants on vacation
        Hundreds of miles across our beloved nation

Pol 8: Acids and metals burning in our soil
        Affecting drinking water and destroying our land

Enter **Pol 9, Pol 10**

Pol 9: The quality of life improved by electricity
        Generates man's need for kinetic energy

Pol 10: Amongst the western world nations play at profitability
        The thought of nuclear fission is a major decision

Pol 9: No time for procrastination.
        We must not hesitate

Enter **Pol 11, Pol 12**

Pol 11: Our natural resources are slowly diminishing
        Scientists are now discussing nuclear fission

Pol 12: The consequences evident are very, very relevant
        We must consider detrimental liability

Politicians 1-12
        The consequences evident are very, very relevant
        We must consider detrimental liability

Enter **Judge** [*Steps down from the rostrum and takes centre stage in front of the politicians.*]

JUDGE: [*Manic.*]
        Amongst the western world nations play at profitability!
        Power plays, environmental games declaring in a unity!
        The sands of time erode away with soil and ambiguity!
        For what is right and what is not they self inflict delinquency!

Exits to rostrum with a flourish.

Enter **Pol 13, 14**

Pol 13: Since European settlement we are the worst nation
    For habitat destruction, land degradation

Pol 14: Salinisation, nutrient depletion
    Australia's major one, environmental concern

JUDGE: Thank you, Australia. It appears evident that you are fully aware of ecological development. Your attempts to remedy the land degradation and salinisation problem is commendable.

Exit all pompous politicians.

HIGH COUNSEL: Your Honour! They must consider less harmful pesticides.

Enter **Dr Sciencestein**

DR SCIENCESTEIN: Ah yes. Some pesticides which are the Western World's saviour from starvation, initiate other problems, such as killing off all living organisms in the soil.

Enter **Bugs** *mingling. Dr* **Sciencestein** *occasionally sprays bugs with a spray can or crop duster.*

Ecological Crawl

    Stick insect. [*Plays air guitar.*]
        We're the bugs that hold the soil together
        Without us there wouldn't be a land
        Pesticides are killing off our brothers
        So come-on - and kill the can

        Life is all
        Do the ecological crawl

Extinction

Dr Sciencestein *sprays bugs.*

Bugs *begin to show signs of distress.*

    Salinisation in the soil's a hazard
    Acidification doesn't help our cause
    So, come-on and get your act together
    And - do the eco - logical crawl

    Life is all
    Do the ecological crawl

    Life is all
    Do the ecological crawl

    We know you need to eat and feed your brothers
    Unlike the third world; you have it all
    Be careful you don't destroy some others
    Needed, needed in the soil

Crop duster

    Life is all
    Do the ecological crawl
    In olden days the land was left fallow
    It had a rest and we enriched it all
    Getting ready for a harvest festival
    We'd have a party, and then we'd have a ball

    Life is all.
    Life is all we need
    To do the ecological crawl

    Life is all.
    Life is all we need
    To do the ecological crawl

Exit dying bugs.

Enter **Old Woman** *Carrying a bowl - attempting to catch rain.*

OLD WOMAN:

> We are completely done for
> Our Kings are gone.
> Destroyed.
> Not one left for warmth or shelter
> Sodden earth, swamped in rain
> Curdling to the estuary
> Marine life gasp, they gasp
> They gasp!
> For pure salt water

Slide 35: Burnt Sand in Kuwait

NEWS PANEL: SPILLAGE OF CRUDE OIL. FACTORIES SPEW POISONS INTO RIVERS. INDISCRIMINATE KILLING OF MARINE LIFE IS THREATENING FISH POPULATIONS.

Enter **Child** *Hand feeding from a bowl.*

Enter **onlookers.**

Enter **Old Woman**

OLD WOMAN: Give it to me.

CHILD: No! No.! It's mine! It's mine.!

OLD WOMAN: I need it more than you!

CHILD: No, you don't, it's mine. [*Child breaks free.*] *Exit.*

Exit Old Woman chasing the child.

JUDGE: Very disturbing indeed. High Counsel, when did this occur?

HIGH COUNSEL: It is ongoing your Honour. But mostly since early 1990.

JUDGE: In view of the evidence presented before me, it is difficult to ascertain where to lay the blame.

HIGH COUNSEL: I agree Your Honour. We have a Catch 22 situation, although men are responsible for their own actions, they are powerless to prevent such tragedies from occurring without cooperation and unity from other nations.

Enter **Sciencestein**

JUDGE: It is imperative that we discover what will happen if men continue in this way. Dr Sciencestein could I have your future projections please?

DR SCIENCESTEIN: Certainly, Your Honour. By the year 3000 our future generations, our children's children have hard times ahead. As I see it . . .

Dr Sciencestein *sits with the world panel.*

Slide of Infertile Land

Enter **Young Man** [*Raves like a madman, coughing between sentences struggling to breathe; he is delirious.*]

YOUNG MAN: Look at those trees. [*Pointing to an empty space.*] Amazing. I tried to warn everyone. They wouldn't listen. Thought I was crazy. Most of them are dead now. They said, don't worry, there are heaps of trees. But they were outsmarted, weren't they? All that lovely poisoning trapped inside earth's atmosphere got too much for the trees and they became toxified and died. Too bad eh! It's only a matter of time for us all.

Lost my Mind – *Rap*

>Here I am sitting on the ground
>Not one tree to be found
>We need wood to cook food
>It looks good, feels fine
>I think I've nearly lost my mind
>
>When I find a galapagos they taste as natural as can be
>Geneticists made them up especially for me
>They taste good – feel fine
>If I had a drop of water, I'd make a cask of wine
>
>The earth stripped bare is unnatural as can be
>Soil salinity is a problem we can see
>The air's thin for breathin' in
>Think I might choke again
>Woah. [*Dramatic death.*]

Enter **Matchstick Girl**

MATCHSTICK GIRL: Alas poor Yorick, I knew him well. [*Gasping.*] Can't breathe – must get into the air dome.

Enter **1st Man, 2nd Man and 2nd girl** [*using breathing apparatus.*]

1st MAN: [*To Matchstick Girl.*] Aren't you a sorry sight.

2nd GIRL: [*Pointing to the dead man.*] Look at him. He's an even sorrier sight.

2nd MAN: Someone burst your bubble?

2nd GIRL: [*Taunts Matchstick girl.*] Would you like this apple?

Matchstick Girl desperately attempts to get it.

1st MAN: Don't waste good food. She's not going to last much longer anyway.

2nd MAN: Come-on. Let's have some fun with her.

2nd GIRL: How would you like to join us in our ecosystem? We've got plenty of food and water there.

MATCHSTICK GIRL: Please!

1st MAN: We don't have to eat pomatoes or winged beans. We've got real fruit and even flowers and trees.

MATCHSTICK GIRL: What do you use for fuel?

1st MAN: There are still a few minerals left in Antarctica. Our next target is - Outer Space. Mars maybe . . .

2nd MAN: What have you been doing to survive? Struggling are we?

MATCHSTICK GIRL: I do my best.

1st MAN: She does her best. [*Takes Matchstick girl's hand.*]

2nd GIRL: Come-on. It will only take a few minutes and we'll be home.

Exit all men and girl..

Scene Futuristic *Two people enter walking in opposite direction toward each other.*

Enter **1st Futuristic Man, 2nd Futuristic Man**

1st FUTURISTIC MAN: Wonderful day.

2nd FUTURISTIC MAN: It feels chilly to me.

1st FUTURISTIC MAN: Why do you say that?

2nd FUTURISTIC MAN: Everyone's saying it..

1st FUTURISTIC MAN: There's trouble in paradise.

2nd FUTURISTIC MAN: Yes. There's trouble in paradise.

Exit all futuristic men.

Enter **1st Man, 2nd Man, 2nd girl, Matchstick Girl.**

MATCHSTICK GIRL: This is a wonderful place. It almost reminds me of earth before its devastation.

2nd GIRL: Yes. We've managed to survive.

2nd MAN: In the early 20th century when Earth's fuel resources became depleted, our scientists and politicians decided to use nuclear fission.

1st MAN: Of course, our technology is far superior today.

2nd MAN: We've been operating successfully for years.

1st MAN: [*Aside.*] If she scrubs up and survives, we could keep her.

Emergency siren.

LX Strobe continues throughout dialogue and song.

People *run around in panic and confusion.*

2nd MAN: What's happening?

Enter **Passer** *by.*

Enter **Saddam**

PASSER: Run for your lives.

1st MAN: What the — hey you. Saddam. What's going on?

SADDAM: [*Evil laugh.*] We have melt-down. You cannot escape. ESCAPE!

MATCHSTICK GIRL: I thought it was too good to be true. [*Strikes match.*]

Times Past – Melt Down - *Matchstick Girl*

>Have you ever thought about how it was?
>Many years ago
>When children worked and children died
>Slaving for their families
>Now children laugh and children play
>Growing more intellectual everyday
>They have everything our forefathers never had
>Opportunity and choice
>
>Cruel times ahead
>Cruel times before
>They were in the middle
>They were the lucky ones
>
>Have you ever thought about how it was?
>Many years ago
>Like a wheel in circular motion
>Heading for a crash
>
>Cruel times ahead
>Cruel times before
>They were in the middle
>They were the lucky ones
>
>The sands of time are changing
>To - an ever-distant song
>Need is not the requisition of the day
>But - want desire and greed
>Destroying of what's left of humanity

FX ECG beep, gradually slowing.

Slowly dying.

> Cruel times ahead
> Cruel times before
> They were in the middle
> They were the lucky ones

Struggles to breathe. Dies.

FX Flatline.

JUDGE: What do you think will happen to the world leaders Sciencestein?

Enter **Dr Sciencestein**

DR SCIENCESTEIN: I predict they could escape to the next eco-system via rocket or spaceship. They would need to be at least 100 to 200 kilometres from Chebar for possible survival.

HIGH COUNSEL: Conjecture your Honour! Sciencestein cannot be serious.

Dr Sciencestein *explores the courtroom and participants with a magnifying glass.*

JUDGE: Time will tell. Time will tell. Democratic Counsel, do you have any further comments regarding these allegations?

DEMOCRATIC COUNSEL: We are endeavoring to reach the people by advising them to reuse and recycle. We cannot take the blame if they will not listen.

JUDGE: Theocratic Counsel?

THEOCRATIC COUNSEL: God is watching us. His presence is near.

LX Energy beam to indicate supernatural presence.

FX Loud roaring wind.

VOICE OVER: [*Powerful voice.*] For there exists hope for even a tree. If it gets cut down it will sprout again. And its own twig will not cease to be. If its root grows old in the earth, and in the dust its stump dies, at the scent of water it will sprout again. And it will certainly produce a bough like a new plant. *(Job 14:7)*

DR SCIENCESTEIN: Hmm! $E = MC2$

HIGH COUNSEL: All rise.

All *stand.* **Judge** *remains seated.*

JUDGE: From the evidence presented before me today, I hereby sentence the world to labour for life. Reuse. Recycle. Plant trees. Deforestation is allowed, however, only under proper management and through the Dept of Environment Judiciary. I therefore adjourn this case for 20 years when the matter will be looked at again. [*Stands, bangs gavel.*] Once extinct, gone forever.

ALL CAST: Remember! Once Extinct – Gone! Forever!

Blackout.

FINALE

LX Surreal

Enter **all cast.**

Harmony

    See the world blue and green
    Spinning round golden dreams
    Precious gifts are given to you and me

Extinction

And since time was begun
Of this world, we have one
We should live in harmony

No one should be in need
With no war or greed
Be my friend, in the end ,sow the first seed

God is watching us here
And some feel he Is near.
Let us learn from all - of our past mistakes

It's the hope for us all
We should heed nature's call
And live in harmony

Acknowledgements

National Geographic – various
Brundlandt, G.H. – World Commission on Environment and Development.
Pope John Paul II Quote "The ecological crisis is a moral issue."
Dr Hewson: Improving and Protecting our Environment.
Department of Prime Minister and Cabinet: Ian MacLachlan's Office, M.P. Member for Barker; Robyn Mills Electorate Secretary.
Hon. Susan Lenehan, M.P. Minister for Environment and Planning.
Shadow Minister for Environment and Planning, David Wotton M.P.
Office of the Minister for the Arts, Sports, the Environment, Tourism and Territories Nicola Head – Assistant Adviser and Gerry Morvell – World Environment Day Eco Facts and Quotes.

Bibliography

St James Translation of the Holy Scriptures: Genesis 1:29, 30
Proverbs 10:14; Job 14:7
Bulletin July 10, 1990 National Geographic – various
Pope John Paul II – Quote – "The ecological crisis is a moral issue." Head, N & Morvell, G., World Environment Day Eco Facts and Quotes.

Extinction by Lynn C Campbell 1992
First Published in Australia in 2025 by
Carole Campbell Writer carolecampbell390@gmail.com
All rights reserved.
No part of this publication may be reproduced or transmitted in any shape or form, either written, copying, recording or by any technical means without the prior consent of the writer or publisher
ISBN:9 781764 298803
Carole Campbell Writer
MA. Writing & Literature, Grad. Dip. Ed.
Produced in Australia 2025

www.ingramcontent.com/pod-product-compliance
Lightning Source LLC
Chambersburg PA
CBHW081237080526
44587CB00022B/3976